Peter's Story

My Mum and Dad are …

Lynley Barnett

 A catalogue record for this book is available from the National Library of Australia

Copyright Text: © 2023 Lynley Barnett
Copyright Illustrations: ©2023 Helen Iles
All rights reserved.
ISBN: 978-1-922727-72-5

Linellen Press
265 Boomerang Road
Oldbury, Western Australia
www.linellenpress.com.au

Dedicated to Peter

This is Peter's story. Peter just turned 8 years old.
For all the Peters in this world
who don't have the words to use to make parents listen.
Here is what he wanted his parents to know.

You may not know this but:
I worry that I am the reason you divorced. I have tried to be good, did I do it all wrong?
　　Was it my fault?

I do need you to reassure me
and talk to me in words that I can
understand. Sometimes a hug will do.

Sometimes I think if I had Harry Potter's Wand I could make magic, and we would all be together again. Sometimes I just wish.

Please, please, don't make me choose between you. I can't do that.

It scares me so much because then you might not love me, Mum, or you might not love me, Dad.

I want to love you both.

And while I am talking to you both ...
Please don't say nasty stuff about each other. I can't shut my ears. I hear what you say and it hurts me so much.

When you shout, you scare me.
I don't know where to hide. Please,
please don't do that.

And do you know I hate being asked a million questions when I have been to stay with Mum or Dad. I feel awful answering them, it's like a quiz that I can't get right, no matter what answer I give.

I don't know what to say. I don't know if something should be a secret, and you get so angry when I just tell you what a good time I had.

Don't you want me to have a good time? It is so nice to just play with each of you, or curl up with you, like I used to do.

I want to use my phone to talk to my Dad, or Mum. Please can I do it privately.

I don't like my conversations being overheard. I'm not talking secrets, just privately.

Yes I may say stuff about you, Mum, or you Dad, and sometimes just because I am grumpy what I say comes out mean. But usually I forget about that the next day.

I never ever want to carry messages from Dad to Mum, or Mum to Dad. It's horrible. I never get that right either. I mess that up and then I get into trouble, big time.

 You could have a book with messages in it about my sports lessons, or my music lessons, then I wouldn't have to remind you. That would really work.

I would like a programme, just like we have at school where I know what classroom I should be in, and which teacher is with me. The programme tells me when I am going to see each of you. That way I understand what clothes I should wear and when to be ready to go.

Sometimes I leave behind some of my clothes – please don't be angry ... I really don't mean to do this, it's just that I forget.

Please don't say nasty stuff about my dad's family, or my mum's family, because I like my Nanas and Pops. And I love my cousins. I miss them. They are my family. I have known them since I was a baby. I like being with them.

There are other people who ask me questions about us and I answer them, because you have taught me to be polite. I don't know if there is something I should not say. It is so confusing.

I talk to my teachers too and they help me when it is not a good day. Is that OK?

I know I have come back late from visits to Mum and to Dad. But if you shout and get angry I want to run away and hide and just never come out again. Did you know that?

Is being late my fault too?

There are things I will never understand. One of these is about Money. That's only for Grown Ups to discuss, and you have to do that when I am not around.

I know you get unhappy about Money but that is work for my parents, not for me. I'm still trying to do school sums.

There are sometimes when I am sad for no reason, and when that happens all I need is a little bit of your time. I like to be protected and safe and being with you while you just listen to me, even if you and me both don't know why I am sad. And it's okay if you share hugs with me.

I know sometimes you are sad, and I promise to give you the best of hugs to help you too.

Do you know what I would like to help me to grow up strong and secure?
   I would like my two most special people to just be kind to one another. To just be sociable, to make decisions about me that means I am going to spend happy times with Dad, and happy times with Mum.

My life changed when you two divorced. But I am strong, and I will live in two different houses, and see two different families, and I will love them all. I know that love is something I have a lot of and can share really well, but you have to help me.

You have to look at this from my height ... and I am way down here.

   I make mistakes because I am just a young person. I know you make mistakes too, so I forgive you your mistakes, but, there is a condition ...

I forgive you, Mum.
I forgive you, Dad but you both have to forgive each other just a little bit, so that I can grow up into a happy person, one that will make you proud of me.
Please, can you do that?

About the Author

Lynley Barnett spent many years working in Perth WA as an A.D.R.P. (Alternate Dispute Resolution Practitioner) or Mediator to you. She worked thousands of hours in Mediation, with adults, couples, and businesses.

She wrote this book to help children whose parents are divorced or divorcing.

www.ingramcontent.com/pod-product-compliance
Lightning Source LLC
Chambersburg PA
CBHW051320110526
44590CB00031B/4420